AS WATER MOVES

ROGER MITCHELL

DOS MADRES

2023

DOS MADRES PRESS INC.
P.O. Box 294, Loveland, Ohio 45140
www.dosmadres.com   editor@dosmadres.com

Dos Madres is dedicated to the belief that the small press is essential to the vitality of contemporary literature as a carrier of the new voice, as well as the older, sometimes forgotten voices of the past. And in an ever more virtual world, to the creation of fine books pleasing to the eye and hand.

Dos Madres is named in honor of Vera Murphy and Libbie Hughes, the "Dos Madres" whose contributions have made this press possible.

Dos Madres Press, Inc. is an Ohio Not For Profit Corporation and a 501 (c) (3) qualified public charity. Contributions are tax deductible.

Executive Editor: Robert J. Murphy

Illustration & Book Design: Elizabeth H. Murphy
www.illusionstudios.net

Cover: detail of "The Islands at Port-Villez", Claude Monet, 1897, is in the public domain.

Typeset in Adobe Garamond Pro & Cochin
ISBN 978-1-953252-93-7
Library of Congress Control Number: 2023945875

First Edition
Published by Dos Madres Press, Inc.

For Dorian
Again

TABLE OF CONTENTS

CONTOURS

ONE-LANE ROAD

MESSAGES FROM KEPLER

LETTER TO MAIRA AZAM

AS WATER MOVES

CONTOURS

SOMEWHERE IN THE MIDDLE CONTOURS
OF THE LAURENTIAN EVACUATION
AS IT VEERS NORTHWARD
FROM THE UPPER HUDSON DRAINWAYS

We live between two rills
and south of two others.
We did not plan this.
It happened like a shrike
happens or a stray cloud.
All four converge in what
beavers made one year
a pond. This was before
we came here, before
the map was drawn, on which
the rills lie like thin hairs
from some river otter
rumpling its way past.
On the ground, they lie
nothing so keen or clean
as a symbol or thought,
as readable landscape.
Though it is thought these rills
provoke at times, these small
determinations of
the grade or gradient
or gradual travel dirt,
the earth, seems to insist
is its reason to be.
To move as water moves,
filleting crevices
in the composite body.

It is down the same pour
every mountain slides
bit by bit over its
unendless millennia
and into which we place
our rabbity skitters
and deep slumberous strides, on
whatever down we make,
river we take.

*

After a rain, after a steady
drizzling day-long downpour
slashing through the neighbor's trees
like thunderclouds fleeing
their own releasing. Water
cuts its own course through rocks
washed clean by constant run-off,
down nameless rills,
dry in the dry times,
a crease in the hill above us.
My neighbors, the ones
who live here now, we
who live here now, those
who don't and may never,
who park their money on the land.
A slope that if you climb it
turns into a ridge.
Up at its low point, a pass,
a place cleared long ago
for logging, part of an old road,
now abandoned, steep,

rising between Lincoln Mountain
and Pine Hill, where it joins
Number Five Brook
till the brook turns northeast
into the swamp at the upper end
of Natural Dam, and the road,
here a path, there a brook,
reaches the flat col
between Bluff and Little Bluff mountains
to the north and Beech Ridge
and Death Mountain to the south.

*

You need a map to get there,
though you can find it blind,
walk across or through it
and not bother with names.
You can live not knowing,
in dents in the earth,
on hills or slight rises,
slanted and nameless, place
where your eyes pass across
as you go out the door to the days
of your life, somewhere
in a ripple, on a hump
along a shallow slant between
two elevations, at the edge
of what's possible, where
the earth paused before passing on.

*

The swamp, the great swamp
at the headwaters of Number Five Brook
packed tight between two humps,
Black Ash Mountain to the west
across the top of which loggers
opened a savannah with high canopy,
a pleasure park to stroll through,
and to the east Hog Back Mountain,
truly in back of, north of, Bluff.
The two, Black Ash and Hog Back,
holding like a geologic pincer
the high flat ridge of Natural Dam,
through which the melting glacier
cut a deep vee, draining its slush
west into Number Five Brook
and east into Kelley,
making Natural Dam the last,
lowest arbiter, determining which water
flowed northeast into Lake Champlain
and which went southeast
into the same. Two local watersheds
feeding a long thin lake.
At its north end, the Richelieu
takes it north into the St. Lawrence
and out into the North Atlantic,
past St. Pierre and Miquelon,
where in spring it laps the sides
of meteoric blocks of ice
floating south
out of the melting
High Arctic shield of ice
that, were it to survive,

would keep life
more or less
as we know it
for the few hundred
thousand years
or so we
are allowed
to be.

A DREAM (WOMAN IN A WHITE CAR)

I was having a dream
in which I had to walk from one supermarket
to another
because I owed the one I was not in
six dollars
and the one I was in
didn't want me to eat any of the scallions
I had bought there
there.
So, I rebagged the scallions
and, remembering that I owed the other supermarket
six dollars,
began going through my wallet
and discovered in it a new type of money,
a sort of padded bill
that also served as a kind of open envelope—
for carrying money, I suppose—
and as I had a five and a one
in this strange currency,
I left my groceries in the one store
and ran across the parking lot to the other,
almost getting run over
by a woman in a white car,
and when I reached the other store,
the store I owed the money to,
I thought, this is silly,
I should have brought my bag of groceries,
which I had already paid for,
with me. Even in the dream I thought this,
and, as I was turning to go back,

someone called my name,
someone whose voice I recognized
from the world outside the dream,
someone real.
I turned to see who it was
and was just beginning to make out a face
and a waving arm
in a crowd of people in a checkout line
when I woke up.

I do not know who it was, even today,
never will,
but someone I knew,
from a long time ago, I think,
reached me, as they say, by dream.
I'm not the kind of person who says this kind of thing
easily. Or ever, really.
I tend to be suspicious of dreams,
maybe just annoyed with them,
since they all seem to be about the same thing.
Anxiety, frustration, a world
that won't, as a parent might say, sit still.

I've come to expect things to be
pretty much the way they are.
I don't need wings
to fly out over the night
or a wave to rise up in front of me
with its blank brow,
and I suppose the reason I stay with
this dream, let the words
slide easily across the page,

hoping they might coax
the voice I heard and the face it belongs to
out into the open, is
that the voice was real to me,
that buried in the slurry of the dream,
the ridiculous padded money,
the running back and forth between two supermarkets,
the scallions I couldn't wait to eat,
was a real person,
a person who had known me long ago
and remembered me as I was then,
a person who if we were to meet again,
in a supermarket,
even a real supermarket,
would call to me,
call out to me, even,
and whatever person I had been then,
which I have difficulty remembering,
he would greet me in the joy of finding me
and we would talk amazed
for fifteen minutes or so,
each of us bringing the self back to the other,
self we had sloughed off somewhere in the past,
self no longer useful in the world
or plausible even,
but once, as I say,
real.

I realize
that the real person in this dream
might also be a fiction,
no more real

than padded money,
that it was to get me to see the real,
the real itself,
that reality, perhaps, is not the same as the real,
that the dream served up the fiction
of a person from my past
who, when it came time to say,
my god, you,
disappeared.

Outside,
two total strangers
bat a tennis ball back and forth
across a net.
This is the condominium complex
where my mother spent her winters
with people like herself
who long ago decided that reality
was a few things practiced
in an emptied space.
I can't tell who's winning out there,
or if they're playing a game at all.
In the late afternoon haze,
two people seem content to disappear
into bounce and counterbounce,
into crouch and lunge and swing.

Today,
I am having another dream,
only this time I am not asleep.
I am looking out the window
of a house in the mountains

and trying to imagine myself here in these mountains
forever. Looking out the window,
summer and winter, at this field,
which now, at the end of November,
is covered in gray sky and a thin layer of snow.
The mountains in the distance, though small,
have their tops buried in cloud.
Like dream, cloud takes whatever shape it wants,
including none at all,
and, except for that,
never repeats itself.

A raven passes the window.
I can tell it's a raven and not a crow
by the slowness of its descent,
by the ease with which it rides the air.

Yes, I did say "forever,"
but you know what I mean.

ONE LANE ROAD

THESIS

> *" 'Tis certain, that the mind, in its perceptions,*
> *must begin somewhere."*
> —Hume

The mere presence of a book of philosophy
makes me lean toward it. I grip the squared block
of reason in one hand, and it settles me.
As the cowboy settles the straddled bull
between his legs. I know what you're thinking,
and you may be right, but we have to begin
somewhere, even if it means a trapped
animal has to throw us to the ground.

HERON MARSH, PAUL SMITHS

It's likely I came from a place like this.
The silken muck at the bottom of it
feels like an early attempt at skin
along the inner arm. The tiny bugs
on the water's surface flash like a thing
about to break into thinking. The tufts
of last year's grasses, cattails blown apart,
I know that raspy clatter of wisdom.
It looks good on the page but tastes like dust
if you utter it. I'll take the moss
that curls to itself and never leaves home,
lichens that grow on rocks. And, of course, rocks.
Broad, level, varied, this place gives water
a break from all that rushing out to sea.

WE HAD SET OUT

We had set out, as they say in old books,
so long ago, I had now to invent
much of what happened, then salt it
with some that did, such as the day
we were coming back from some event
up north, Raleigh or Chapel Hill,
one of those family outings made
to hold in place a limitless free rambling
someone would call, when the rest were gone,
the way it was, the way we saw it,
the way it served up the ebb and flow,
that I saw out the window, head held down,
trotting its way back down a two-lane road
in 1946, the dog we had been told,
for reasons clear at the time, we had to give away,
reasons I can't even remember now,
miles from where we were soon never
to be from again, determined to return.

WHEN THERE WAS LIGHT

I have now the Bible of a woman
I never knew, Ella Davis, who had
her picture taken at Frederick's
Knickerbocker Family Gallery,
whose motto, just off Ninth at seven seven
zero Broadway was "et facta est Lux."

Ella is the aunt I wanted years ago
to guide me through the narrows I was in,
a hoarder who never bathed, Mother said;
Aunt El, whom no one but my mother
ever mentioned, and that only once,
as I was poling through a gaudy swamp

of poets and their misery. I love
the brooding dawn of another day.
The light changes so slightly it can't be seen.
A woman wants a likeness of herself,
a moment caught like nothing ever is.
She takes the train north to New York, to Frederick's.

And there she is, still. Looking, not at us,
but at some secret hope she thought the eye
of the camera might see, since neither God
nor man was taking notice. Buried deep
in the pebbled leather of her Bible,
small gold letters whisper Ella Davis.

THE SILENCE

All around us forgotten knowledge stirs.
My father almost never mentioned his,

whom I discovered died of typhus
in the great epidemic of 1918,

a man who was mentioned only as he
who died of cirrhosis of the liver,

who wanted to be like his father,
a doctor, who wouldn't allow it.

Too hard a life in the days of horses
and buggies. Calls for help at any hour.

Dead at forty and later buried
where his father was the following year.

Who may have given his son the disease
that killed him, working to save a few

of the tens of thousands bringing death
back from France. Then died of it himself.

Or of grief at having killed his son's wish,
and then his son, the man whose jacket hangs

in my closet, a white flannel sport coat,
"1901" blazoned across it in red,

who it was said became an engineer,
and someone his son rarely mentioned.

In the last census he answered
he called himself a salesman. Of what

he didn't say, perhaps wasn't asked.
Last fall, on a visit from my cousin,

she told me that years ago her mother,
his daughter, told her she heard,

at eight, quarantined with him,
his last choked breaths,

heard the rattle, when the mouth
can't swallow its own saliva.

That would have been enough for me
never to mention, never to want to,

had I been there. As, for some reason,
I want to imagine my father was.

How full the silence must be,
that so little is remembered.

MY OLD KENTUCKY HOME

"The sandman am a comin'
to my old Kentucky home."
Something like that. We never had
an old or any other kind
of Kentucky home, but when she sang,
it seemed as real as traffic.
In a later and less marveled life,
I lived so close to Kentucky
for so long, I never went there.
Everybody has that kind of Kentucky,
I think, a place so big and near,
so full of a kind of wonder,
you don't need to go there.
It was that place in the song she,
who never married, sang me to sleep with
on occasional nights in New Jersey,
so many years ago I can almost touch
her old, even then, electric toaster,
the sides of which came down like wings
on a model pterodactyl, a flying wedge,
that must have flown through sizzling piglets
to bring back such blackened toast.
My old Kentucky home had a front stoop,
not a porch. You wouldn't want to sit out
quite so close to so much traffic, even though,
across the highway, a barn peeked out
from behind what had been a farmhouse
so long ago it looked like Moses slept there.
My grandparents lived there in their huge
overstuffed recliners, couches, ottomans,

accoutrements to the life, hardly Kentuckian,
they bathed in like waters into which
you might insert quietly, behind drawn
curtains, all you dreamed of being
at the end of day when the sandman
set out on his rounds from Kentucky,
the North Pole of sleep, scattering
the dust of obliteration over all
the little New Jerseys of the world
where the toasters hissed and spit in the fury
of transubstantiating bread to ash.

AN OLD IMAGE

Two boys in leggings, the kind wrapped
around the calves of soldiers in the first war.
Officers had leather boots in that war,
privates and non-coms, cloth leggings instead.

Facing each other at ease in a foxhole,
their helmets on the ground beside them, one foot
bared, its big toe stuck in the trigger guard
of the rifle each had been trained to fire,

the working ends of which rested under their chins.
They were Nisei, Japanese-American boys,
who volunteered to fight Japan, anything
to escape the relocation camp they'd been thrown into.

A photo taken on Guadalcanal in 1942
and printed (no comment) in every American paper,
which every boy in America could stare at
and see the point of, that it wouldn't matter

that the mothers of these boys might also
one day see their sons dead in a hole,
caught going AWOL forever, squeezed
between two world orders neither could abide.

GARDENS

All that mulching, plants to tend, weeds to pull.
The Japanese Beetle, something called wilt,
the wash-out rains, the early freezes, rot.
Sitting on the porch in the evening, fine.
Watching dew drop out of the sky. Fireflies.
The smell of dirt. Under your nails. Dirt soup.
Some of the soups I've had, a few I've made,
still had the grainy edge, the smell, of ash
scattered over the winter, the small stink
of rotted potatoes, cabbage leaf, the grounds
of endless cups of coffee, mother mud.

With Dad it was model railroads. He filled
a room, or started to, with a plateau,
plywood, around which little engines of his youth
would carry loads of airy coal and lumber,
wheat and cattle, to pretended markets.
You had to crawl on hands and knees to reach
the hole at the center of that world.
From which you ran it round and round for hours,
or would, once it was finished. That Eden
collapsed under a load of disinterest
on my part, since it was mostly for me
the little world we were making was built,
or begun. I was twelve, already gone,
self-expelled. No need for the dread angel
with wings, two of them, as big as a door,
and the road already paved and waiting.
The child trying hard to be a man
or what he thought a father ought to be,

now that he was one. Getting to that station
just as its train, crammed with strangers, pulled away.

It must have taken days to dismantle,
pulled nail by pulled nail, unscrewed screw by screw,
angular slabs of carpentered wood propped
up against the wall, later hauled away,
given perhaps to some other luckless dad.
I make the whole undoing up, partly
because it happened, had to, and partly
because undoing is a native skill.

I went somewhere. Most likely to my room.
Where winds and storms and blind oceans blew
across continents of strangled branches.
I couldn't mount such things in the tight closet
of toy trains and their zippy spins around
a track, crashing sometimes onto naked
plywood, still waiting for its hills and trees
and probably houses with people, dogs
standing stiffly, waving at the silly train
that never stopped, except when the gods, us,
tired. And what can it mean when a god tires?
I was not one, and I was not tired. Relieved
of such archaic duty, I went back
to tinkertoys and homework, he,
to saving the world from spit-borne parasites.

Though these were Edens, too, small gardens
by the roadside made of anonymity
and wonder and a mighty need to be.
Including the mighty need to leave.

PULLED TAFFY

Svetlana Filipovich, doyenne
of my first, fumbling boyhood
hormonal rush, onto the lips
of whom I pressed a
hesitant kiss in the hallway
outside your door before fleeing
back into the safer weirdness
of my incomprehensible loneliness,
nursing it with nightly walks
on the boardwalk where the ocean
kept sanding the voices of the lovers,
lovers I was sure were out there
in the dark (though the word "lover"
had yet to enter my available
word hoard), I want to say that I meant
to come back, though not,
as you see, in person, but in poem
(another word unavailable
to me then) and not immediately,
not the next day on the beach
or the day after that at the shop
where they pulled taffy
shamelessly in the window,
but here at the end of two lives,
only one of which I've heard of
in all these years. He's all right, by the way,
and he wants you to know that many times
in the intervening decades, in the tremors
and slidings of the average earthly visitation
he has sometimes repeated your name:

Svetlana, Svetlana Filipovich,
wondering who you became
and whether your parents, whom some Germans
tattooed along the forearm,
survived the innocence and the taffy,
and the hot stinging sand of south Jersey.

CAB RIDE

She stood beside a stack of boxes
at the curb, guarding all that was left
of a life suddenly blown apart.
The dispatcher had warned me
her voice was shaky on the phone.
She said she had no one to go to
and less of an idea where.
I told her The Sunshine Motel
had low rates and no interest
in anybody's history.
Fine, she said. I helped carry
her boxes into the unit, trying
not to pry, but still let her know
by smile, tone of voice, mention
of the weather, that I cared,
even understood. I couldn't,
of course, but I knew something,
something unforeseen, terrible even,
cruel. I wanted her to know
what I wanted to know myself,
what I knew I would someday need,
something so foolish I blushed
saying it, even then. You will
survive whatever it is now
you think you can't. And, hoping
to arouse some intractable force
on both of our behalves,
I thanked her for the tip
but gave it back.

In Boulder,
nineteen sixty-one, when even
the world didn't know what it was,
she took a taxi like a pill,
passed the memory of it on
to someone who thought he had seen
what it turned out he had,
an intimation of the slow
adjustment to the curb, eyeless
faces flashing past, little
but the minute in your pocket.

"WHY DID GOD MAKE NETTLE?"

Molly, age 5

The poem doesn't know what it wants,
but it knows the minute it hears
the boot on the floor, the catch in the throat.

It watches to see if the snowflake stops
in mid-air. It cheers when the afternoon
falls. It dreams of tomorrow and kisses

it gladly goodbye. It doesn't ask if
God made nettle, but it praises the child
who, when it stung her, wondered why.

GRIFFY, DRAINED

A thin stream slivered through the drained lake,
the spine of a snake, curled in a long bowl
of dirt, the banks washed clean as a dune.
Where were the stumps, the stunned branches, the barn?
Where was the lank shack of the rain?
Along the edge, the stranded lilies groaned.

A can of rusty beer at the bottom popped.
The sweat of the boy who drowned last year
lay close to the lip. And a name like low fog
drifted over the tight mosses. I slid
down in on the cracked mud and raked
among the corpses, happy as a crab.

It was a slice of melon in the dark
down there, the moon turned inside out,
the earth undressed. When they pulled
the blanket of clear gray water
up slowly over the emptied valley,
light twitched as the fish leapt up.

for Richard Hugo

ON THE SLIDES

We live in a camp.
—Wallace Stevens

Almost spring when a cloud of Cedar Waxwings
drops onto the Maple, poses for twenty seconds,
then at some hidden blink of the sky explodes back into it.

At the far end of the field, Connie and Will's barn
continues its slow implosion, its nightly complaints,
the wailing of nails drawn slowly out of the barn's body.

The road we live on, named for the farmer who tilled this field,
not the loggers who opened the forest, nor the surveyors,
we have it mowed as part of an invisible contract,

what somebody once thought was the right way to bring a coffin
over a mountain or place it in the ground at an angle where
the exchange of the two dusts could be made and the
    gatekeeper paid.

Up in back of the barn, to the south and beyond it, above
    Wainwright,
miles farther west, near the top of Whiteface, its newest scar,
no more than ten years old, shines in cold sunlight on last
    night's snow.

The Slides, as the skiers call them. Only the daring dare to
    ride them,
bucking the mountain down, crack and release,
as sky keeps opening slowly the door to our first home.

MIRROR

It's the way he comes into the kitchen,
partly. Dark T-shirt, bare feet, a forced aplomb.
We are there only as obstacles,
a kind of smiling furniture, set out
to break the space. We are busy with words,
wine, our lives, an opinion of Strindberg.

We are, suddenly, the same people we were
after the last lecture. We are saying
the same thing. The lecturer is saying
the same thing, thank you, and I hear myself
telling someone, stop me if you've heard this.

He fixes a bowl of dry cereal
and takes it off into the house somewhere.

It may be the saying of the same thing
that brings us out. See, I am still here.
I have worn a place down on the stone step
at the side door. I have come and gone,
always returning, always going out.
I am out now, and the stone is keeping
a rough score.

       The tall, diffident boy
in blue jeans and bare feet, hair cut short,
hoping not to catch whatever it is
we are, I wish him better luck this time.

DEAR EMILY

You may not understand this,
safe in your alabaster fame,
but we teach you now. Odd, isn't it,
to think of yourself as Somebody.
Plato and God and Emily Dickinson.
We were talking about this yesterday.
It was an introductory class.
They were new to poetry, I think,
and I came close to saying, This is why
we're here, here in this room, watching
an imaginary fly buzz by.
We were talking about death and the folds
in the many garments you made for it,
and how it arrived, or rather, stopped
kindly. I have to tell you, it didn't work.
The valves of their attention were shut.
The few words they sent my way rolled
into the corners like dropped marbles.
You see, one of their own had died
early that morning. It was on
the local news. A sudden
unpredictable carrying off of a kind--
well, of a kind that was not kind--
that did not dazzle gradually,
but tore like lightning through the roof,
and truth, like an uninvited guest,
roamed freely among the rooms
fingering the mind's worst fears.

DRINKING WINE ON THE DECK
IN LATE AFTERNOON DURING THE
ANNUAL PINE POLLEN RELEASE

Watching tiny grains of yellow dust
pollinate the surface of the Pinot.
Should I drink them, as the heroes do
in Homer the sesame seeds or wheat berries,
before the slaughter? The day slides off
its robe of light, arrays itself for sleep.
Finer than talcum, the pollen grains descend
on everything, including the letters
of Philip Larkin to Monica Jones,
which I read as invisibly as I can,
and as slowly, here inside the great
green mist that hovers across the valley.
No little ruffle of the leaves went by
without their noticing the owl buried
in shade or indigo bunting doing
its bill wipe on the alder bush. No end came,
too, to their hesitation and desire.

Connie and Will's barn continues its slide
into the earth, stern first. We are at sea,
it would seem, and though sinking, do not move
toward the lifejackets or the folding chairs.
Midsummer turns slowly toward us, shaggy
as a satyr, promising nothing at all,
presenting itself as large beings do,
mastodons or muskox, who lived here once,
and like the old people in a novel,
serve an obscure purpose polishing the bars
of their cell and interpreting the coos

of the lackadaisical dove. A large
swept-winged bug lands on the poem, with twin,
arced antennae and a red tail cocked upward
through the stern cape its lacy wings make.

MY NEIGHBOR JOHN

My neighbor, John, has a sign out front,
half hidden in knee-high grass. It says
he wants a law repealed that I want kept.
He lives alone on oxygen he wheels around
the house. His car is backed to the front door,
just in case. When his dog kept failing to show
last year, I wanted to ask, but didn't.
The last time I'd seen them out together,
Kyra Lee could barely walk. "They rescue us,"
he said one day through his gap-toothed smile.
I never asked what it was he had to be
dragged back from, but it must have been slowly
over crushing disappointment or flung
into a tub of love that never jelled.
I don't ask, and never will, why he opposes
gun control. His reason has a life
I've never lived. It knows needs that aren't mine.
But it knows what rescue is, and that's enough
for me to stop and chat about the grass,
the many kinds there are, how fast it grows.
Like me, he mows it. Sometimes, though, he lets it go.

SUSPENDED LAW

You say you miss not having known me then,
I, who will never see you with a cane
stopping to catch your breath on the third stair.

Back then I barely fit inside my skin.
Days disappeared without a trace.
Disasters I'd have missed had you been there.

Though what I know of memory tells me,
it's days like these, long and delicious, full
as bowls, that don't know what they are, or where,

that follow blindly like a bee its swarm,
like clouds the curvature of earth, some law
of gravity suspended, love like air,

that can't be seen because it's everywhere.
And can't be missed because it's always there.

SHIPMATES

"I must go down to the seas again,
to the lonely sea and the sky."
                    —John Masefield

A few months from dying at eighty-nine,
ankles swollen, a highball in her hand,
Granny brought back from her twenty-something
memory, "I must go down to the seas again."

To what the poet called "the vagrant gypsy life."
The one where you give it all to "the mist
on the sea's face" and "the white cloud's flying."
Not the laundry, the mice in the attic, dust.

She could lift then only her drinking arm
above the shoulder, her husband dead now
twenty years, but "the gull's way and the whale's,"
and a nightly old-fashioned, kept her camber.

The last time I saw her, she said goodbye
so roundly, we could have been shipmates
parting ways in some foreign port, she off
to the Azores, me to the Cannibal Isles.

I managed only a whisper in return.
To a woman who grew up on a farm
in Camden County, but later found herself
in the rollicking staves of a poem.

WATCHING TV IN THE WOMEN'S IMAGING
CLINIC WAITING ROOM

I love the way they play at being here.
They talk like friends who have their lives somewhere
over there, on the other side of the room.
It might be called Belize this morning, Rome
this afternoon. Michael is telling Kelly
about his weekend. Kelly's face follows
along, with intermittent winkings at
the audience.
        This is the moment when
someone pushes the narrow tweezer
into the deadened breast to tear out the rot.
Which saint was it who, mutilated, looked
kindly toward the sky's flat fluorescent glare
and wondered why God had to wear a mask?
The fixed face of competence above her
describes every thrust precisely, how long
each took, while taking it, how many more
there are to go, so she would always know
where the knife was, what it was doing now.

Michael departs, washed in applause. Kelly,
the same. Off to the valley of silence.
An hour of being somewhere on a street,
hurrying. To or away, we aren't told.

WATCHING THE WIND

Lift a small shovelful of snow
      without a shovel
off the stubborn blanket of it
      in the field
and throw it completely away,
      quickly, too,
so quickly you couldn't find it ever
      crawling
on your hands and knees, calling
      out its name,
puff of purest cloud, smoke
      of frozen fire,
wind's breath, you,
      with no shovel
and a handful of white air.

NO OTHERNESS

Winter comes back, a small gray stain, a scar
in the sky above Esther drifting northward,
a cloudy bruise. Long low rumbling of hills
behind which owls crouch waiting for dusk.
The wind throws up a spray of powder, drags
it through the pines. Foxes prepare their paws.
So much has gone back down where things are not
what they are but a shred of what might be.
The woman who walked along the road has stopped.
The grass sleeps in the field. The moths are dust.
We drive down to the river to watch ice
fish for water and the water twist away.
The edges of things turn toward each other
as though there were no otherness or kind.

SEND US A SIMILE

It's the clouds again and the hummingbird.
The shimmering hot air. Air you can see
boiling above the tar shingles. Call it
the second of August, late in your life.
The long stand of white pines behind the barn,
the neighbor's barn, Connie and Will, who sing
a singular song in the falling down
barn of our days. The coreopsis pops
its blossoms under the spikey needles
of the Austrian pine. I've never known
such runagate drunken sun as now slabs
over the disappearing day. O wing,
droning over us now, what is it like
up there between the bee and outer space?

A WALK ACROSS A FIELD

Wobbly path among
downturned grasses,
the dog up ahead,
pilot and guide, finding
the usual clues
to being alive, stuff
to tell from other stuff,
a place to find a way
to want to be in,
like today or a nest
so deep in the grass
you'd stick your whole
nose into it, head and all,
though who's to say
what chances are after
in a world invented
by hunger and luck
and the need now and then
to walk across a field
and not come back without
snowflakes on your sleeve,
the scent of wet leaves.

SOMEWHERE IN THE DAY

A throaty "grawk" lifted out of the wall
of white pines to the south. I waited,
but no response came. None I could hear.
I was fiddling in the yard, picking up
bits of things September had sent us,
the glassy wing of a dragonfly, leaves.

Maybe the Raven talks to itself at times.
Maybe it calls with no expectation.
Just calls. Or needs to hear its own echo.
Makes the blunt forested heap of its home
up on the mountain in back of us say
back to it softly in Raven, "grawk."

A RECEIPT

A gas station just off Germantown Avenue,
the night after she died.
Thirty-nine years after the divorce.

Self-serve, no one around.
Tomorrow, I drive home all day.
Now I watch the numbers climb
on the digital screen.

All my life, counting.

Whatever else it's made of,
it always has a number.
The four sides of the screen,
single car at the corner light.
The sixth floor, 7:45 pm.

The pump stops itself.
7.24 new gallons in the tank.
"Do you want a receipt?"
The "Yes" button smudged
from so much use.
Yes. I push it.
I want a receipt. Of course.
I paid for it.
Of course I want a receipt.

DOCTOR'S ADVICE

He told me I'd better wear a helmet now.
OK, I said. Dad never wore a helmet.
He skied till he was eighty. He made sure,
I think, to ski when he was eighty,
even if all he did was slide a little
sideways across the fall line, stop
and watch the view come into view.
At Winter Park, you couldn't avoid it.
It was always there, perfect, sunny,
everything packaged in white. He said,
you go ahead, Rog, I'll meet you at noon
for lunch. It was lunch, I think, that made
the trip worthwhile. Skiing alone takes
more than concentration. There you are
in all you'll ever know of paradise,
and your father is trying not to die
today by admitting he can't do it
anymore. The people, the ones
who are looking for paradise again,
fly by working their turns. They know it's near
and have now almost left themselves behind.
I'm good at pretending, or think I am,
so I told him I'd see him later,
and I concentrate, or try to,
on the turn I'm in the middle of,
the one where the wind is bending the trees,
the snow, the view, and the distance
things and everything are beginning to be from here.

BROKEN COFFEE BREAK

I stroll up to my favorite out-of-town coffee shop
and find it closed for good. Through the black glass,
naked counter, stools scattered, space thrown open
to conjecture and rats, stillness, indifference.
I came here to sit in the shade of my deafness
in the mingled business of being mortal, the push
on to the next moment, letter I meant to write
once each week for the past four months, knowing
I may not ever, even though the Asian Daisies
are blooming and the cool sheen of morning still
hangs in the air. What perishable milestones
we apprentices have for measuring anything.
Better to take the pulse of the sunlight falling
down over the mountains into the yards and alleys,
the Royal Palms and freeways, the perpetual
serpentine muscle of traffic sliding over the hills
into one's own arroyo or canyon, place to pause
and collect, gather and climb back into
the ceaseless, moving and unmoving,
constant boa of motion. With fine gravelly
contractions of swallowing the delicate morsels
we make in the always and indescribable now.

A PERFECT STRANGER

My exhilaration is always the same
driving down the road. It's as though
I can finally unfurl myself
to the weather, the accidents
of happening, like meeting someone—
a perfect stranger will do.
We ask each other how the other is,
and we both say "fine." We *are* fine.
It was only a few months back
that I discovered cherry birches.
They grow on my neighbor's land,
this a neighbor I've never met,
and the cherry birch a tree
you might also say I never met,
despite its growing along the path
I walk almost every day.
Cheered forward on the simple business,
the complicated overcoming,
of hours, of days, each one of which
is like no other, each a small grain
of some fortuitous immersion,
we say goodbye, the stranger and I,
not really believing in the strangeness.
It was the leaf of the cherry birch
that made me stop, a lance-like spear tip,
exaggerated shoulders at the stem,
but, too, its slenderness and the dark,
shiny, "nearly black, smooth" bark,
as D.C. Peattie describes it
in his book on eastern trees.

OK, immersion, but in what?
Air seems a likely substance, air
that is everywhere, even the ground,
under the ground, where it is pressed
tight to a leaf, a molecule of water,
the shadow of a perfect thought.
The cherry birch "loves the ancient
forest loam, likes to have lady fern
and maidenhair around its feet."
A perfect stranger, it's leafless now.
Along its branches the swelling starts.

THE LADY IN THE LIQUOR STORE

I saw her at the clinic first,
trying not to see me. Perhaps,
like me, trying not to be there,
where they don't hesitate to blurt
out which bit of your wiring sizzled,
which chip blew. Someone has moved
into the empty house next door,
except that it's not next door. It's
downstairs, the attic, the basement.
A bat got in at dusk. Even
it doesn't like it here, hangs up
behind a curtain or bright mirror.
Maybe if you don't breathe, it will
do what you want it to, not say
anything, pretend it isn't
frightened, small, here, a living thing.
Hello again, I said. She smiled,
fist locked on the neck of a bottle.

HAVING TO HAVE

Messy thing, the self. One has to have one.
I watched someone have hers taken away.
It took years. She had to watch, too, from inside.
When the body decides to open
the spigots, release the crystals, one can,
at the least, talk to it, call it by name.
But when the mind begins to leak, loses
its lover, the tongue, yet forces one to watch,
the best she can be is spoken to,
or worse yet, wept on like an open grave.
We buried her above ground, as if to say,
you may not have her, who did not save her,
though who we were talking to, it wasn't clear,
and couldn't be reached or even named.

In memoriam B.C.G.

THE MARCEL PROUST DREAM

I came up from underground this morning
into the small city I lived in once,
every building under reconstruction,
air swarming with sunlight and dust.

Last night I finished reading the fat black
book of Marcel Proust. I watched a life
go past for eight hundred pages, and afterwards,
got up and went into the other room.

In the first five months of World War I,
three hundred thousand French soldiers alone
died. They couldn't have known that at the time.
The delay in living life prevents it,

lets us live first. Then sends it back to us
in pieces, sometimes in dream, a scramble
of intention, vestibules and loss,
air powdery with sunlight and dust.

He was always cold, walked around at night
in a heavy coat. Bombs fell on a street
nearby. Nothing drove him away. Death
became him, that and hounding his publisher.

It is good mothers never know their children
and heaven is a fiction. Better that
the papers lie about the carnage, God
be gone, no one to talk to but Himself.

EXPLAINING

I'm always explaining, explaining
my poems, I mean their meaning,
or explaining why I wrote them
in the first place. Often, and frequently,
it is the first place I'm explaining,
as though that would explain why
I was there rather than beach combing.
That things seem to need so much
explaining might explain why so much
gets so little of it or gets only a part
of what, without even asking,
it asks for. It makes me wonder
what it would be like to be in a place
where everything was explained or,
by strange coincidence, or no
coincidence at all, cleared the decks
of all consternation and bemusement,
turned explanation itself into
a dense tautology of wonder.

NATURAL DAM*

*A geological oddity in the valley of the east branch of the
Ausable River, Essex County, New York

When we went out looking for it,
having never seen such a thing,
when we stood not far from the place
on the map where it said it was,
when we shoved about in the bush
looking for anything like it
and scrambled up a hill to see
if it stood off from the place marked
on the map, the spot we stood on
looking down, and of course it didn't,
and so gave up and went back
where we came from, back to doing
things I now remember only
by doing them, one of which, slow
to elbow its way through our brains,
years in the making, laggard as growth,
was to go back, slave to an itch,
and find that the hill we'd stood on
looking off in the distance
for the thing was the thing itself.

For Hanns Meissner

HUMAN EFFORT (after Jacques Prevert)

Human effort is not this beautiful young man
        smiling/ standing
on his leg of plaster/ or stone/ dispensing grace
          to the puerile artifices of the
              statuary/ the imbecile illusion/
of the joy and
          jubilation of the dance/ evoking

with his other leg in the air/ the sweet gentleness
         of a return
home/ No/ Human effort does not carry a small
          child on the right shoulder/ another there
              on the head/ and a third on the left shoulder/ with
tools slung across/
          and look a woman hitched to his arm// No

Human effort has no true home/ stinks of his work/ has
          trouble breathing/
his salary is scrawny/ as are his children/
          Human effort has no manners/ human
effort is a child/
          is as old as barracks/ prisons/ churches/

as old as factories/ everywhere he has planted
          all the vines// fed
himself on bad dreams/ is drunk on the sour wine of
          resignation/ like a drunk squirrel/ spins
              dizzily/ in a hostile universe// forges
without knowing
          a chain/ the one by which everyone

binds themselves/ see misery profit labor carnage/
          sadness hardship
insomnia ennui/ the terrifying chain
          of gold/ of coal iron and steel/ cinder
              and coaldust/ strung around the neck/ of the helpless

world// where also
        bracelets, trinkets, medals, artifacts hang.

The sacred relics/ the crosses of honor/ medals
        of old servants/
trinkets of misfortune/ the great equestrian portrait/
        the great gilded likeness/ the grand full-length
                display/ the big visage of the large thinker/
the high leaper/
        the dignified and sad prankster/ dictator/

liberator/ aggressive pacifier/ the head
        of the firing
squad/ the firing squad of your country/ of mine/
        detainer of those without legal recourse/
                elected/ head of the massacre/ cheered in the streets/
protector/ Of
        a thing that slipped off under the crowd's roar.

THROUGH HARKNESS TO PERU:
An Aria of the Epidemics

> *Harkness: a Scottish surname from the Old English Hereca, the
> first syllable of which means army, plus the Old English næss,
> headland or cape. Peru: a Quechua Indian word implying land
> of abundance, a reference to the economic wealth produced by
> the rich and highly organized Inca civilization that ruled the
> region for centuries.*

I was driving the back road through Harkness
on my way to the doctor in Peru.
In the season of worry, I was sick
thinking of the dying already done,
the dying that was to come, arbitrary
or deliberate, it hardly mattered.
I thought of cab-drivers, I thought of nuns,
people who look at clouds, count beetles
or the number of steps to the front door,
or wish on a star with one eye closed, want
something to happen before tomorrow night,
walk along a road looking for grass blades
and trash, wish they were pretty, wish they
weren't as pretty as they are, lack enough
calcium in their bones, can't see what the point is
to anything but moonlight and fast cars,
find themselves suddenly pregnant, rush
out into the night to meet it, pray
by scratching a place at the back of the skull,
hum in contrapuntal harmony with the river.
These are a few of the losses suffered
driving the back road through Harkness to Peru,
looking for something that language knows
but keeps bottled in the stammer jar.

Escaped slaves spent days dreaming in cellars
off this road, so they could be alert at night.
It says so on a sign, though you have to stop
to read it. Some do, I think. And one year
Russian Razorbacks broke loose from a farm
near here, called back to something remembered
but taken from them. Also hunted down with dogs.

Along the road in a stand of trees, the land
slopes down to a patch of water, water
in a creek, water at the edge of a pond,
where someone several years ago, no one
I've ever seen, because I go by there now,
on my occasional doctoral rambles
just to see if this time he/she might be
sitting on one of the stones arranged to be
sat upon under one of the trees, but no,
never have I seen who it was who started
and over time, years to be exact, began
where no one lives, a garden now with path
down to the water and later flowers
planted with small stone edging here and there
placed to make nature approachable and kind
to the eye, anonymous and rare
as the gray fox crossing the lawn last night
with its tail bent down in concentration.
And no doctor to go to but tomorrow.

CONTRIBUTOR'S NOTE

It wasn't the poems I turned to first
but the notes in back, the pressed tissues
of a life. What was it poets did
besides write poems? The poems looked fine
spread out on clean white sheets, Olympias
in full stare, Odalisques, their eyes lowered.
The ex-fisherman from Nova Scotia
wrote grainy poems with full imprecision.
I imagined thick mist and cods swaddling.
Another got her poem taken
by swimming the English Channel. At night.
It crawled across the page in long, sure strokes.
I tried posing in front of the mirror,
also at night, naked in fact. But, no.
It wasn't English Channelly enough.
I took up boxing, tried being fetching--
"Drove a Duck up the Alcan Highway drunk,"
"Once mentioned lunch to the Duchess of York."
The editor, though, said he knew the Duchess,
her butler I think, told me my poem stank.
So I stamped my passport harder. "Rafted the Nile."
"Held the door open for Melina Mercouri,
who taught me that dance, the one where you step
sideways and stop, then step the same way back,
arms over shoulders, the bouzouki in tears."
I never went back to the front matter
where the pale lemons lay in studied space,
where the poet sought so hard to minimize
his garish adventures, jobs in Djibouti,
hikes across central Asia, Gobian

hallucinations. The original
fantasy, the setup, the platform,
was better than any rocket it launched,
the place where the poems were born,
inventing a life you'd live if you could.
"Published his first poems at twelve." "Sat in
after hours with Monk at the Blue Note." "Wept
to see Kennedy die, over and over
in reruns, King have a dream he'd never live
to see, the rest of us never as well."
That's what I call a little bit of hell
that you and I are living through. I wish
us well. I always will. But "Jesus,"
as my grandfather said in tight places,
as we waited to hear what miracle now
Jesus was asked for. But he never said.

THIS MORNING

To not make it more ornate than it is.

Would be an Amish sort of thing to do.

And, as there was a black boxed buggy shoved
horse first into a hedge at the far end
of the County Court House parking lot,

I could mention refusal as an informed
motion of the mind,
                                    should there be a want
of that kind wanted,
                                    as in I refuse
to be in the same world as was present
to the senses yesterday on CNN:
Distortion, denial, lies, two dead nuns,
mass killing of children, dogs left to die.

A turning away from, a giving up?

Lack of specificity leaves room
for everything.
                        Not knowing what to think
when what you thought mattered
                                                        is no more
                                                                                is
the new contaminant in the water.
Utterance
                sticks
                            to the roof of the mouth.

For a while I tried imagining how
an Amish farmer might have passed himself
through the Court House metal detecting frame.

Sideways seemed right,
                    naked maybe,
                                singing
something strange we used to know the words to.
Nothing but his beard to trip the buzzer.

CLOUD FORMATION

For a long time, and without knowing
what he was doing, that he was doing
anything he or another could name,
he came to see that he had been trying
to put something back into something,
something from which it had been taken,
something to which it had belonged,
removed when he wasn't looking,
possibly by himself, or borrowed
while he was away, or his mind was.
The clouds passed over, and the thing
kept not going back into the place
out of which it came, where he thought
it belonged, where it seemed to fit.
The clouds couldn't say what it was,
perhaps misunderstood the question.
They kept their customary aplomb.
But for one brief moment, panicked,
he thought it might not have been
what he thought it was, or where,
that he lived somewhere above the clouds,
in back of them perhaps, over there,
and so, of course, it wouldn't go back
into anything he could imagine,
wasn't what he thought it was, wasn't
even he who was having these thoughts.
It was something else, and the something
it went into was as well and now lay
all over the sky like a parachute
that opened too close to the stars.

EDGING WHILE LISTENING TO THE RADIO

The morning and the Northern White
Violet hiding in the shade of a blade
of grass. The same morning foreign workers
in Abu Dhabi were stacked three high in slums.
The sun will spend all day in the sky while
I spend most of it edging, digging a trench
between the roses and their enemies.
Everyone seems to have them these days.
A woman whose husband killed their daughter
and then himself has now lost her mother.
My dog lies in the sun, his eyes closed.
I think he has no enemy but me,
who will not give him plates to lick all day.
It never was a world you could live in
for long without some help from ignorance.
The dog depends on me for everything.
It feels like love, the kind you grow in a small,
boxed garden outside your door, the only bane
the Cabbage Moth, the Japanese Beetle,
and dirt, dirt you keep having to coax away
from its fascination with the weed,
the weed that needs almost nothing--water,
sun or shade, or, for that matter, dirt--
just unspeakable spit and fury.

ONE-LANE ROAD

Away from the rattle and skerve,
a single lane of dirt and gravel
never plowed in winter. The sun
drops quickly through cold air
giving the scattered stumps
and ratted slash
left by the loggers glisten.
A torn-up place with
some of the shine of human
effort left behind.
Even the dog has found
a fragment of rotted bone,
and I have mine as well.
I get to be with the earth
again and my certainty
that I know so little
about it, except that it's
always dying and always
coming back, and has,
like those it leaves behind,
no idea not its own.

SOMETHING REFUSES TO MATTER

It could be the pile of sticks next door,
or the piles of papers on the dining room table,
piles of varying sizes and heights,
stacked in a way to suggest that something
was meant or intended
but is as yet unrevealed,
born in the mind of my neighbor, and in mine,
or given my neighbor to mind
by himself perhaps or the neighbor before him,
or in the case of the papers piled
on the table at which
it is no longer possible to dine,
allowed by me to accrue

and wait.
       But for what?

I note the slant of the thinking,
the hasty shape of the stacking,
the needful grouping of like things in a group,
as though the two of us knew
we could move only a few things forward,
that life saw to this cautious economizing,
this hobbling,
promoted it as a check or balance
to the giddy velocity of certainty and rapture,
and we would have to leave
whatever it was these piles might be found to mean,
or be,
       to you perhaps,

to bring nearer to a human shape
where one thing follows from
another. Not follows, follows from.
As looking at a pile of sticks
follows the piling
and the leaving of the pile there,
to be looked at, considered,
made an object of contemplation and wonder.
And later, I'm sure,
      no, certain,
burnt.

NOW THAT I'M OLDER

Now that I'm older than Wallace Stevens
ever got to be, what do I say?
I'm sorry? That's what I said to Dad
when I saw him last, laid out on a stand,
or table, in the back room at the mortician's.
Maybe that's why I said it. I knew then
I had forgotten something, maybe
how I got here. You can't just
drop out of a passing cloud or thought,
though I love saying it. Maybe I did.
Maybe that's what I want to say
now, to Wally and the rest of the gang.
I'm sorry, but I've stopped being sorry
anymore. The wind is blowing the way it does
when everything before it, clouds included, bows.
Not to it, but to the way it's going.

THE CHINESE HAVE LANDED

Seventeen below this morning, the moon
over Esther flat and artfully blotched.
We never see the other side of it.
The elongated downcast bearded man
across the aisle stares at, possibly through,
his knees. The woman beside him looks sideways
at her device. She, too, can't watch TV.
I sit under it so as not to see it.
A woman in a wheelchair, pushed in
by her son, is whisked away at once. Not
to wait in a waiting room arouses
speculations, though no one speculates.
The garble of laughter and comment does
the thinking for us, piped in from somewhere.
Surely, the weather, when they get to it,
will be local, and what's more, bearable.
Meantime, we have the picture on the wall,
the ceiling tiles, the strange dismal fabric
of the surgically matched furniture.
Across the room, even facing the TV,
the son has dropped his head. Let him sleep.
The glittering efficient inner rooms
await us. The masked proficiency
of everything near the end. The nurses
with homes and mortgages, even tattoos,
hand us off to others like bags of sand
against a rising river, holding back
the tide, or when the bell rings, easing us
down into it. The sun is out there shining.
The Chinese have landed on the moon's back side.

I can't wait to hear what it's like there,
when for the first time light of a new kind,
ours, will shine where light never has.

TO THE PEOPLE OF UPPER BLACK EDDY

Whoever you might have been back when
it was decided the bend in the river
was the place. Water curls in on itself,
blackened by the upper canopy of branches
or muck scraped from the sodden sediments
and slopes that dampen the Delaware.
A counter current to the larger, more
insistent, thrust. Many must have passed, pulled
along the towpath the makings of a life,
where now a small twist of tar humps over roots
in the roadway between houses clawed
to the hillside and those wedged up against
a defunct canal. Those who now live there wait,
arrange small bits along the river's edge,
a thought or two, something accrued,
sweepings time draws across one's estuary.
How good to be among the residues
and trailing weeds. I stopped to ask the way
to Tinicum in Frenchtown. They thought I meant
New Hope, and so by misdirection,
I found an inside edge instead, a selvage,
this catch in the swallowing we swim in.

RIVER SWIRL: OTTER CREEK

The rubbed sides of
invaded pools
pull back
a counter whirl
in the fluid branches
while the whole
muscled shaft
shoves forward
sucking little
circular sips,
whirlpools of air
at the surface,
kissing the passing.

We sat by the edge
eating a sandwich
hearing the low
notes in the swollen
grumble of stone
passed over, turned
and rolled
over like bones
in a boiling, licked
by millennia of silt.
A spittle of suds
nudged the dirt
at our feet
as though washing
what no longer
needed it, never

stood outside itself,
beside itself,
as an eddy would,
collecting
the slicking
of riverthought.

ABOUT THE DREAM

The clouds float sleek and low over the hills
without moving a muscle. See the bee
approach the umbrella and swerve away.
See the nuthatch. It may come to a point
we can't believe, but hasn't it always?

The idea of the other, for instance.
Something keeps clouds from crashing to the ground.
Call it what you like. The word doesn't know
what you want it to be about, nor does
the something that keeps avoiding the word.

SOMETIMES THE GRASS

Sometimes the Monarch butterfly,
which goes past in a manner
no other thing has thought of,
not even the day, or the cars
hidden beyond the trees,
which pass so as to leave
constantly on the air
the sandy noise of their going,
I want to say nowhere,
since the noise is constant,
but nowhere doesn't exist,
especially if you live there.
Sometimes the grass waves,
and the lanky clusters
of yellow flowers bob
in a way I'm beginning
to imitate, though if the wind
is gentle enough, they sway
instead, singing to themselves,
and the grass sometimes listens,
and sometimes doesn't, content
to be grass sometimes,
but sometimes prefers
to dance the way people do
when the curtains are drawn
and nobody's home but you.

NOTHING/NEVER

The freezer sits in a corner of the garage,
broken and bereft, being very quiet.
For eight years, it's been like this.
We need to get rid of it. We broke it
by leaving it in the garage the winter
it dropped to thirty below. Who knew
a freezer could not stand being cold?
Must we always be careful, sensible,
paying our bills on time, looking out
for the safety of the world, plus
the safety of those in the world, those
like us who don't read the directions
on every product to the end and put
freezers in safe dry places like garages
where, wonder of wonders, they freeze to death?
And then leave them there for years, each year
of which we say in passing, please make it
go away. It hath no freeze to give.

We cannot, though, say it gave nothing.
Nothing may come of nothing, as Lear warned
his loving daughter, but Nothing gave us
time in which to pass and years to measure by.
We've had these eight years, or is it ten,
to marvel at the wonder of evasiveness,
skipping past an obligation, years on end,
delaying duty like death itself, saying,
not now, maybe next week, exploring
the possibilities of never, but never
telling Never, You may not play at our house.

MEASURING

I have lived more days than Mt. Everest
is, in feet above the sea. Though the sea
is rising, which means Mt. Everest
is shrinking. To climb the whole mountain now,
as we found it in our tiny time on earth,
you will have to start beneath the sea,
somewhere off the Ganges delta, ankle deep
in ashy water, lapped by who knows whose
thin residues. Days and feet, whole mountains,
oceans, rivers, human waste. They are ours
to measure and be measured by. I've heard
the sky is forty billion lights years out.
If only we were light. But, then we'd have
no feet. Or days to smolder into ash.

DIRGE FOR A DYING BARN

They call it the middle distance in books about
looking, but this was Connie and Will's barn.
It's gone. Clawed to the ground over
three days in May by a spindly backhoe.
You could hear bones crunching across the field.

I wanted this barn to be always falling,
frozen in going down, with a light wind
soughing across the grass bearing the scent
of rust, hand-made nails, and locally planed
planks cut from trees dead loggers spat on.

It made a way, a quick way, of looking
at most matters first thing in the morning
as marginal but gritty, permanently
transforming under the pressures of light,
then dark, and then, slowly, the light again.

If there is a kind of lamentation
or way to thank the feral cats, the mice,
this place for which a small white owl is named,
the many moanings of the suffering roof,
desiccated shakes covered in rusted tin,

I cannot think of the anthem, hymn,
or ritual, the utterance or wail,
high-pitched enough or long-lasting enough, so,
send a hissed "yessss" to the wild grape and vine
that wrapped it every summer in its leaves.

ENTERING THE GENOME

Someone stumbled
into a middens in Mississippi,
a hook and a twist
                of what looked like fiber.
        *

They found a bone under an Alpine glacier,
a gift of global warming.

        *

Under a parking lot in Leicester,
            the maligned spine
of the last Plantagenet.

        *

The DNA comes back
whispering secrets
            you can't connect
to anything you know.

        *

Unless it's the whole
            swollen passage
of human history.

        *

                Though maybe, too,
the part that one day
wandered away
            into another life form,
a different cul-de-sac,
swarming with grubs and bits of bark
            living under rocks
in the Gobi Mountains,
                which are now a high flat desert.

*

Or the worm that found a way
      to break
into a molecule of snow
and suck its marrow dry.

    *

And, too,
      may never be discovered,
      never known.

    *

Which is, after all,
only a human thing.

SKYLESS SKIES

"Life has no purpose."
—Sloterdijk

Life trips us up like luck, or fleas.
Can wobble, wander off, and will,
leaving us devoluted, drawn
into prey for some future phase
life has, I almost said, in mind.
Life has no mind, just pure thrust
outward, as we go out each day
hoping to concoct a reason for
the Dodo, not to mention life.
Which is not us, but uses us.
Not even uses, passes through,
as wind the grass, as cloud the sky,
as sky the skyless skies of space.

LITTLE WAVES

Nothing will survive, nothing we know now
or will later on, when the earth goes back
into its elements and their capacities,
free of us and our meddling, antecedent
to our being, witness to our having been.

See the little waves slide up the shoreline.
They want nothing more than to come aboard,
then go back out and try again. I love
the little waves that found a way to do
the only thing they were capable of.
Fall on the sand. Then do it again.

I don't mind that it's cloudy today
and the wind is a little rough.
The ribs of the palm fronds tell the wind
which way to go. Over there, they say.
I can't see where that is exactly.
To be honest, I'd rather be here
listening to the happy clatter
the fronds make scratching the wind's back
as it blows down the coast, boisterous, off
to some ruckus in The Society Isles.

JUST SHY OF BEING

This world is not conclusion
A species stands beyond
Dickinson (501)

The bobcat strode straight across the small field
in back of us and up onto the stone wall.

I shouted downstairs to Dorian. She
got there just as it struck a determined line

across the moss and with no fuss or fear
disappeared into the woods a neighbor owns

but never visits. Another who stays just
shy of being among us. Or, possibly, one of us.

LIFE: A WORKING DEFINITION

Asked by NASA to come up with a reliable definition of
life that would work in any situation, a panel of scientists
said in 1992 that life is "a self-sustaining system capable of
Darwinian evolution." Not quite, said David C. Catling
twenty-one years later. Here's a better one: life is "a self-
sustaining genome-containing chemical system that has
developed its characteristics through evolution." But on
17 May 2016, Mitchell wondered, wouldn't it be more
accurate to say that all self-sustaining, genome-containing,
chemical systems capable of Darwinian evolution are the
products or versions or manifestations of life, not life
itself, not the deep core of that idea?

Life being an idea,
like a tree. Life
being also a word
        for an idea
signifying something
of which we are voluptuously
        and hideously
aware
but barely understand.

Maybe understand,
but can't explain,
language being what it is
and isn't.
        Quick
as spit and slow
as bad weather,

life
is like the wind.
We never see it,
only what it brings
and takes away.

Only what it's like,
never what it is.

An originating force to a variety of forms,
unlike any of them,
yet inhabiting them all,
not ethically or with extended physicality,
but simply as the pure will
and capacity to be
what it always and only is,
alive.

Cannot exist, perhaps,
apart from its not-quite-self-sustaining manifestations.

A container and its content
            both
            brought into being
by and only by
joining one another.

Or, more likely,
has no problem existing
apart
from everything
we can know
or reach
by language.

REUNION OF STRANGERS

Yesterday, I went out into the world,
and as often happens on days like this,
there was poetry and rain and a long drive
in the car and people who had lived
so long in their own worlds and been
so long themselves the world seemed
invented just then, unaccountable
and just like it was, gathered next
to a river rushing against its banks
so hard and fast the stones quivered.
Who were they to have lived so long
under a mountain, away in a valley,
way off in a life like mine, and why hadn't
we met, or did we, and did we forget
when we went there? Yet there we were.
It was like a reunion of strangers,
of people we'd never been or known,
but people we knew we would be
one day and be glad to come back
to the place we left before the river
began and the town slid and the rain.
It was an afternoon, and we all looked
at each other like we knew something
it was so hard to know, and so old,
it was new, though we'd always known it,
and again, still, couldn't say what it was.

BIRCH

BIRCH

Bricolage: *The process of improvisation in human behavior; a work made from a diverse arrangement of things that happen to be available.*

I went into the little grove
by the pond one year
and stood there.

I was looking for marsh marigolds,
clusters of deep green leaves with yellow blooms
that live by water,

but I had stepped into a cage
of white light.
All around me

arrows from the sun
stuck in the ground
flashing their feathers at the sky.

*

In Old German, the word for birch is "bark."

*

The wind blows across the field
snow on top of snow
a liquid slither of dust
the color of the paper birch,
peeling.

*

All around us, forgotten knowledge sleeps,
as Snow White slept, remembering nothing.
When she woke, she was unchanged.
She couldn't understand the leap
in the Prince's joy, that she had died
to him
and then come back.

*

Birch is one of the runes. A mark
like our capital B, the Roman B.
Not a letter. A character,
a symbol of something valued
in a world discovering that thought
could be held still for a moment,
passed on as a made thing, a mark,
without which all could be lost. This,
when the written word was a door
into mystery, a "secret discussion"
in Old High German, a poem
or song, invoking a source
or fund of imaginary honey.

*

We make a fire in the wood stove
two hundred nights or so a year.

One year we burned birch, our birch.
Two hundred days a year making ash.

First father and then mother.
Ash is the last.

It floats on the air,
feels like grease.

Which we learned trying to give
some of mother back to the sea.

It blew back at us. As though
she had forgotten something.

*

Before the Greek alphabetas
reached the north, far from Sanskrit and Linear B.

When writing came upriver or over the mountain
from dark places. The first meaning of rune

is mystery and magic. Writing meant you could see
sound, touch thought, keep it bundled in scratches.

In cultures of the north of Europe not yet
overrun by Greek and Latin urbanity and reason,

but soon to be so, Birch,
tree of the north, tree of snow,

paradoxically, tree on which you could write
once you agreed to have the magic

of written things and live by its laws.
Its laws, not the laws written on it.

Or, if you were still a creature of long winter nights
and the two bright eyes watching you from the dark

edge of the woods, or the love of losing yourself
on a bushwhack so you could find your way back,

a language of rhythms and scrabbling, of going
out to the end of what you were and knew,

what you carried to your last inward breath--
a place where language staggers and falls apart

or into one of those brilliant transitional phrases
Bizet put into *Carmen* that made love the lover

of anything it looked into the eyes of long enough.

*

Each rune had its own rhyme,
a small song, the music for which is lost,
hence, for which new music can be found.

Without it, and the saying of it,
air would fall out of the sky, water stop
dead in the river, stone turn to ash.

*

"Leafy twig,
little tree,
fresh young shrub."

Three strong syllables
holding things fast
here and now.

First to return to a wounded forest,
thing of beginnings,
light in the hand and mind.

*

Once I disturbed snow buntings on their nesting grounds,
not meaning to do so, in the heat of my own
and different love of flight to the far north,
the isolation of the musk-ox. What that is,
I still don't know. Here, when I see the swarm
turn all at the same time, flashing its white
underwings, and drop into my neighbors' birch,
their ailing, old, lop-sided rhinoceros birch,
their bitten, barnacled, bow-legged sailor birch,
new-leafed in sudden buntings, and un-leafed
as quick, I see where I am. I steady
myself. Though no more than a hair on a leaf.

I fly into the tree of my distractions,
its branches flinging outward and upward,
anything to get away from the torn, blistered,
worm-eaten origin, trunk of gnarled wisdom.
I think I was meant to migrate, but not in the way
of the buntings, who do it only at night.
steered by the earth's geomagnetic wand
tugging them left at a stray cloud, right at rain.

The way of the birch, then, famous for bending,
swinging, at one time, though also for birching,
hunting for disturbed ground, ash after fire,
canopy opened by logging, turning it back
into platforms for wind, light, a second,

a third, a fourth, forest, some migrating hours,
afternoons brushed by the liquid rattle of birch leaves,
returning only as shapes on a page, snatches of song.

*

    …runic delusion
bundled in scratches

      or a liquid slither of dust

         things that happen to be…
going out to the end

         two bright eyes
watching

         no more than a hair on a leaf

anything looked into the eyes of
               long enough

MANHATTAN

MY BAGS ARE PACKED

Out on a visit, now it's home.
Back to the back of the field, stones
at the edge of it, woodshed, stump,
accoutrements to a plain way
of doing things, a way I thought
might straighten the grain or loosen
the knot or lessen what was heaped
against the door, allow a flow,
follow a wing out to its edge
and over. I was right, but it still
hasn't kept me from wanting crush
and release, flight into the city,
the other and wilder other
we are when we're together, thrown
like an avalanche at the earth,
scavenging the day for glitter
and purpose, finding it glanced
like one building off another's glass,
people shoving into a subway.

LETTER TO BERT STERN

I don't come down into the city just
for coffee and a bagel at Shalom Chai,
for a little pretending to belong,
though as the sign inside says in large letters,
it is under the direct supervision
of Rabbi Pinchos D. Horowitz
(Chuster Rav) and often patronized
by small clusters of the local Hasidim.
Nor do I take the long slow train ride down
along the Hudson, so close to it ducks
look up in wonder, geese seem interrupted,
to listen to the laughter and complaint
of people who, I think, invented both.
The Mets would blush to hear what love and hate
they spawn. Death would cower, if it knew how,
to be so starkly ridiculed, defied,
and then like a lover in an argument,
made up to, a lover you hurt terribly,
who knows you'll never make it up, no,
not all the way, not if you live forever,
yet still turns her head toward you at the end.
I watch this happening in your poems now,
Death become someone you have to court,
this time for nothing more than living well.
I listen in on the holy kvetching,
the lyrical arraignment of the end,
hoping to catch the lilt of it, the jab.
You should see the quickness of the cook's knife here,
slicing my bagel sideways. He misses the tips
of his fingers this much, then fills my cup
so full I burn my lip on the first sip.

THEN AND NOW, THE ESSEX STREET MARKET

The person who took this picture took it
well above the parking lot across the street.
"Malted Milk with Ice Cream" cost five cents
once. Leroy's on the corner sold "knishes
frankfurters and root beer," and the cars
and everyone stopped moving for a moment
so this proof could be snapped of the way
a few things stood at the corner of Essex
and Delancey sometime between the Fall
of Rome and now. Which is also falling.

In the upper right hand reaches of the shot,
a line of laundry sags out of a tenement window.
The other end seems suspended in air,
like everything else, both in and out
of the window, the photo, the cowl of dust
that wraps the earth in its own heat. Damn,
said Napoleon, and he turned his horse
and started back across the steppe toward Josephine.

The half dozen newly planted trees lined up
in their iron jackets along Essex were leafless,
so winter must have been on its way, in
or out, we can't tell. The little lie the picture tells
is, though everything is about to change, it brought
life to a halt, so someone could open the door, now,
and let in a large whack of dust and noise,
the kind they make no room for in pictures,
passing them on to the woman in the next booth
who is giving, maybe the air, maybe her mother,

a colorfully athletic lesson in Spanglish,
involving, from what little I can make out,
most of what we call history, as it's apt to look
when the future gets here, and "that fucker
Reynaldo." I have no idea what Reynaldo's crime is,
but, if you are listening, Reynaldo, get over here,
quick, if you don't want to be history.

INSIDE NEW YORK

Across the street
                    and up
six floors, a white

rag wipes the in
side of a window.

The hand that drives
the rag around

the window hides
inside the rag.

SUNDAY MORNING, CHELSEA

A new day at the edge of the precipice.
Across the street, a fire escape scores
a stack of Z's down a building's pocked face.
Popeyes is closed, right next to Earth Cleaner,
also closed. Bags of trash bulge up the sidewalk.
Sunday morning. Consciousness opens
its heavy doors, pulls up to the curb,
drags the reluctant dog past the window.
It sniffs the trash, then lifts a leg
in a salute to rubbish. An ambulance passes,
headed home from a night of putting
the pieces that want it back together again.
A garbage truck erases the view
out the window. Two guys riding it grin
flinging bags back-handed into its maw.
A corporal in the army of everyday
resistance hoists his backpack
onto one shoulder, stuffs his cargo pants
with a few tools of survival, extra
napkins, bags of sugar, swizzle sticks,
and sails out onto the sidewalk, tossing
a glance at the man jockeying his walking
wheelchair with what's left of his legs into
this rescue mission by the side of life.

EREH, WON

The geometrics of empty
                lights
left on all night.

Twenty stories down,
one steady black ladybug
                umbrella
slides along the sidewalk.

                Above,
on slick glass
                two blocks west,
sent down from some
                        unseen
height behind me
                in reverse
c2 – 03:2.

LIKING IT HERE

I

A kind of cosmic finality comes
across the grass with the westering sun
to be a thing to draw down, lean against.

The least forgivable of nature's faults,
its disappearance. To me
who has no stake in the matter, beyond
thinking he would like to think he was part
of a thing that wouldn't simply vanish.

The Taj Mahal, which I have never seen.
The terminal moraine near Martinsville,
which I have, and have crossed going both ways,
north onto the glacial plain, and south, down
along the White River. These are my friends,
two of them, with whom I share the ride,
an entropic slide, can we say downward
on a gravitized globe, since everywhere
on it is down.

I like it here. The dinosaurs were giddy
in their day. The cockroaches look forward
to a less-crowded, more garbolic future.

But they, too, scamper smoothly through
the universe, wait out their time in walls,
foreseeing nothing, since to do so blunts
the will to hunt. Meanwhile, we grub and hoe
our little plot of dirt, our piece of sky.

II

As we enter the nursery of extinction bare-handed,
fashioning the necessary tools out of what lies around,
who's to say this is not, too, to be thought of,
as a "heaven" under construction.

A heaven of the next ten minutes,
a heaven of looking out the window
at the clouds, at the shapes of the movements
of the clouds, at the shadow
of a cloud draping itself across Whiteface
      and Whiteface slowly
        slipping it off,
as all the clouds in Wallace Stevens,
folded forever in the white pages of a book,
          unfurl in the mind of John Ashbery.

          And look,
even in the mind of one placing on his prunes this morning
a cloud of yogurt to activate his bowel.
        In a room of noisy guests
eating and talking,   a modest guest house,
in a city slowly sinking,
      where the crash of it, the isolated phrases,
      make you want to be, not just in it,
but the crash, the isolated phrase itself,
millions of people.

III

The sun pours a translucent green light
over the shriveled foetal leaves of the sycamores
behind the library,

whose imagined roots
decorate the subway walls beneath,
ladders of glass above
take a picture of.

A LULL

I came out of my lighted cave,
blinking with jerry-built wisdom,
headlines eating the sidewalk,
nothing to chew on, no sow's ear
to fill with silken promises,
and there, like a spread blanket, day
lolled on the grass, waiting. For what,
it couldn't say. People lay
all over it, dogs sniffed and peed.
A man looked up at the sky
where the trees held their annual
gathering of leaves, beetles and birds.
The air managed the secrets
of the moment by keeping them,
but too by keeping them moving.
Some stood, struck. Others strolled
in a manner suggesting small
wavelets lapping a lakeshore beach.
Nothing was happening, and so,
continued. Though nothing has only
the instant to move in, never
the hour or day. Even the park
attendant sat in one of his spry
green, collapsible skeleton chairs,
one of which an old Black lady
used as a cane as she dragged it
to a better vantage, from which
to observe, or possibly make,
a more floral arrangement
of the median amicability

which came and went with the same smile.
Everyone seemed to have someone
or be someone themselves, but none
knew anyone in any way
that made the moment skittish
or wish to leave. The purity
of the anonymity carried
the float forward, but so subtly
as to make it seem it wasn't
merely another day, merely
a stumbling old republic
caught in the arms of forgetting.

A TRAIN AT NIGHT

I pick a seat on the waterside, a window
onto what will only be strings of scattered lights
across the river, little shoreline shacks with docks
or up on the bluffs or the set-back slopes, small squares
of white from the picture windows of the fifties.

The river whispers to itself nearby,
invisible, moving in a hundred layers
on its single persistent widening downward
trestle to the harbor and the seaward currents
and the scavenging winds like those I sometimes hear

above the house in the broken spruces and pines,
snapping branches, a clacking like mating gannets,
trees that have been there longer than people, those
who thought living under the ridge or above it
might be the right place to assemble their bones.

I love the lives of other people, and when asked
if the seat next to me is vacant, say, of course,
but dive down into the river of argument,
stream of narrative I'm in, wondering, if this
might be enough books to have pored over for clues

to the silence. I sneak a look at the book
my neighbor has hauled out of his pack. At his face, too.
I can't read either. One of the bright fingerlings
swarming toward the world. I sit silently beside
him and his open book, looking at the window.

In it, my face shadowed, a few sleeping bodies
across the aisle, a glint of light on the river,
the mountains I don't need to see to know they're there.
Remote presences lean away from us, lure us
with silence and distance, closed as an unread book.

The conductors doze between stops now, the last stop,
its rows of wooden houses and high-backed shops flush
to the walkways, named for the river it sits by.
Three people get off under orange light and walk
separately up the hill and into the dark.

Twenty minutes away from the last station,
and the engineer, nearly delirious, lays
long wails of the horn trailing over the valley,
though somebody's driving a car alongside us.
An escort maybe, a pilot ship, a guide.

We slide like a boa into the station, each
lugging something, ourselves, as though in a mineshaft,
up a steep set of stairs to the cars and, for me,
a long drive into the mountains, the towns peeling
away till the road is mine and a new day slips

past the old one, past the sleeping hamlets and farms.
The snow by the side of the road still where it was
yesterday morning, though someone is spending the night
up on the side of Giant, the car parked by the road,
for a morning scramble to the top to greet the sun.

PRISON IN THE MOUNTAINS

I bring a pine cone in a sack. I bring eight.
I say, let's take a look at something simple,
something always around. Let's start
with what's right there, a thing on the ground.
But we're not on the ground. We're hardly here.
We're where nothing grows that isn't
put here. We're where something took everything
away so something else could take its place.
People brought from lives so far away
the pine cone is a mystery. What is it,
someone asks, fingers already sticky
with pitch. Another says, Don't write poems
about us, ok. We're not here. I say,
rubbing somewhere near my elbow, ok.

NOTES FROM UNDER THE SHELTERING BUSH

I woke up this morning thinking of Broadway.
Not the one in the middle of Manhattan
where I sometimes sit in a metal chair
at a metal table and drink the coffee
I bought at Broadway and 37th.

Don't go looking for it. That's the kind of thing
I would do. Besides, before you get there,
it will be gone, probably changed names
or been turned into a bank branch
or the site of a sidewalk suitcase boutique.

I've just gotten off the train in Penn Station
and I'm on my little march north to 42nd
and Fifth Avenue where I will spend the day
in a room reading letters and journals
of someone I never knew and is dead.

She wanted the impossible, day
itself to stop somewhere in the middle,
the ignorance or innocence come back
out of the trees. It wasn't far from here.
She could see it in a doorway, a glance.

I love this person I never knew. She was
a poet, about the age I was
twenty-five years ago when she died
in Boston. I was born there, near where friends
placed her under a flat gray stone

forty-eight years ago. To put it differently,
she was about the age of my mother when both
she and my mother were alive and living
in this world. I now realize she died
in the same hospital I was born in.

Life is made of tricky coincidences,
some of which we never learn about
and so cannot do any more than play with.
I know that something immense
and immeasurable occurred one day.

It was in my lifetime. It could have been
last week when I was up on the mountain
looking down on the valley I live in now
and wondering how long a life truly is.
I was skiing with people I love

and feeling a trifle loose in the tethers
and obligations to others I was bound by
and wondering as always whether
we will ever survive our restlessness
or just use it to make a fantastic exit.

The Broadway I was thinking of was the one
in the Cotswolds, a village I made a point
to visit once because my grandmother had
and had never forgotten it. I wanted to see
what turned my grandmother into a child.

Or the nearest thing to it a woman
of seventy or so becomes when she speaks
of a place she would happily die in
and knows she can't, never will, but sends
the message out across the room anyway,

the one she lived in at the end of her life
in a tall building in downtown Denver,
thinking maybe I or someone I will meet
somewhere will catch the tone in her voice,
and go there and find the version of life

she was sure had not been lost, the one
she had read about once or heard praised
in a low tone by someone she knew telling
its features or describing the way light
reached it, gently, as though not to wake it.

I was living in England then, one of the times
I could take a break from work. Which time
escapes me, but I went into a pub there
and drank a pint of bitter. I made it last,
chatted with the publican, and then left.

I've never gone back, but recently
an email came to my inbox, urging me
to join a self-guided rambling tour
of the Cotswolds, places like Stow-on-the Wold,
Winchcombe to Stanton, Stanton to Broadway.

They have Footpath Societies there, paths
tramped by Picts that keep The Pict among them.
You can walk where the Isles of Scilly spill
into the Atlantic all the way to
John o'Groats off Pentland Firth south of the Orkneys.

We've almost lost track of the Neolithic.
A few sites of intense but remote meaning
laid out on the land. A long horse of white stone
dug into a hillside. The giant squared pillars
of Stonehenge framing the sun's return.

Under and around these silent monuments
or stones that speak like fragments of sculpture
or broken lines of appeal to lost gods,
the faint record of a people whose walking
was its way of thinking and thanking life

for giving itself away.

It's the dead of winter now and the Jays
attack the feeder one or two at a time.
The chickadees zip in quick between them,
snatch a seed and flit back to the center
of their sheltering bush and start pounding.

It's soothing to think it might be the birds
who outlive us, if anything live can.
I've thought of space, but such a crowd of stars,
and the constant tuning of the ether.
Give me the chickadee and the small seed.

PRAIRIE WARP

PRAIRIE WARP

                              Out

beyond the horizon

                clouds sink

                              into a sea

of air

                show us the great bend

of the earth

                by sending sight

straight off it

                              into space

                                             out

where even the horizon

                isn't

                              horizontal.

OUT ON THE PRAIRIE: DAY ONE

Stopping at a stone,
      its glacial etching,
      its livid lichens,

a flower I think I know,
      but don't,

glancing across a heave of land,
      slaloming down its grasses,

carried by some current
      out and away,

where, before long,
      I've lost the path.

Alone,
      I give myself the shiver
      in a moment's fear
         of being lost.

All that I'm tied to,
      all that I thought I was,
         slips off
      like a cloud
running an errand for the wind.

So that
finding a way back
      becomes the shape I make on my walk,
the gift given,
         out of some buried thing there.

GRAZING THE BOTTOM OF AN OCEAN

Picking over rocks and flowering weeds,
mushrooms and bone fragments, dried dung,
drowning in the acetylene air,
a cluster of Hare Bells pokes through the grass,
and beside it, the five frail petals
of the Skeleton Weed.

All morning, up one wave
and down another, riding slowly in
toward shore, a skull,
still hooked to its antlers,
and out of one eye hole, disturbed
by my bending over it, a butterfly.

BELOW SEVENTY MILE BUTTE

*Gordon Hempton, acoustic ecologist, called Canada's Grasslands
National Park one of the quietest places on earth.*

A breeze finds a way to get between
the new sign and signpost behind me.
All afternoon it makes a tune out of
five or six intricate, wailing tones
with long silences between them and no
need to stop. Or start, for that matter.
The sign and I are the only things here
besides the view, the grass, the miles of sky,
and all that nature hides inside them.
The square of shade I sit in lets me write,
in these words, at this pace, that everything
has its song, and sings it best alone,
in as few words as possible, out here
checking on the limit and its aspects,
listening to the least amount of sound
recorded anywhere, here in a grave
the ocean made out of its last long waves.
A car creeps up behind me, stops. Then turns
and goes back, trailing its rattle of gravel.

A PRAIRIE ROADSIDE SIT

I saw it miles away across the shallow valley.
A road that lifted off the ground
and disappeared into the sky.
That's where I want to be, I said.

Where grasses finger the wind,
pushing an open blowy sound
through the cracked car window
while the wind rolls on its back,
tumbles and twists like bison in a wallow.

A flat-bed semi passes me before I know it,
dragging a long cloud of dust behind,
flashes past, disappears in seconds.
The sky's neighborly whispering closes over it.

JUST AFTER SUNRISE

I write this from some shade
        I had to make out of a rented car
parked at the edge of a field
        at a right angle
        to the sun,
my back to the rear tire.

        About to dot an "i,"
when the "i" moves.

Smaller than the period I make
        with my ball point pen,
it climbs up through a forest of words,
        runs into some heavy brush,
                hops

or flies
        on wings I can't see
        over the word "start"
and disappears.

        The prairie
                spread out on all sides
as wide as sky
        starts to scribble
        another day
on its page.

NIGHT ON THE GRASSLANDS

She can't sleep, so she gets up.
I pretend to sleep, want to sleep,
think if I lie here invisible
she'll at least be quiet enough
to be bored into sleep. I'm not
invisible, and no one
was ever bored into a sleep
they cared about, but I'll try.
If things just get quiet, if I can
possibly stop thinking about it,
let consciousness wander away,
I might just steal a piece of sleep.

"Come look," she whispers. "Quick."
I give up. I come. I look.

Up at the top of the ridge, the crown,
the top arc of a full moon, rising,
no farther off than the owl's hoot,
tinted by the earth's cowl of dust,
a mix of ochre and exhaust
telling us, sleep is an evasion,
dream is real, and behind the stars
silence waits to be awakened.

MESSAGES FROM KEPLER

IN THE BEGINNING

there was no such thing.
Nowhere was everywhere,
and they were the same thing.

As with the beginning, which was not,
so too with the ending.

Eons of microscopic palpitation.
A little dust, a little wind.
A very little water, heat.

A kind of molting.
As a child sloughs its mother
and is later sloughed by another.

Endless morphing toward the possible.
The possible leaning toward,
becoming, but not knowing what.

A stone teaching itself to fly.
The wing beats in the middle of it,
though the stone doesn't know it.

Something else does the knowing.
Something else does the being.

MESSAGES FROM KEPLER, I

NASA sent the Kepler Telescope into space in 2009 to look into one large area near Saturn in the constellations Cygnus and Lyra to search for planets that might be candidates for extraterrestrial exploration. It has exceeded its three-year capability and continues to send back digitized pictures.

("My Name is Kepler")

My name is Kepler, Kep for short.
This is my first report, at best
a jotting. I'm up here staring hard
at a hundred thousand stars.
All day, all night. Three years, at least.
I get my bearing from the sun,
hoping to find a plump planet,
a ripe peach not too far, or close,
to its own sun, cool radiance
capable of stirring the quick
in a biochemical smear,
an extraterrestrial pulse,
slippage of something liquid
at the surface, a wink of water
that in a few thousand eons
might evolve into living forms
not unlike (and here I say, you,
since I'm just a piece of hardware),
on its otherwise barren sphere.
Though hardly barren to other
structures, objects intangible
and inert, stray rays and odd blobs
of light invisible down there,
squeaks wrought by weightlessness brought down
by gravity, vacuum's sharp suck.

What will become of all this junk?
Junk of thinking, junk of wanting.
I am the tip, at the moment,
of your most precious, distanced, pure
intention, but still addled.
What am I doing out so far,
sending messages I can't read
back to people who can't see?
What I do see, I can't believe,
an incoherence, a rupture,
stars, meteors plunging into
one another, into nothing.
Everything turning in its sleep,
as the end of sleep approaches.
Though even nothing has a catch
to it, something that snags something
else, more invisible, lesser
in the long string of apparencies
reaching across vacancies
even the angels abandoned
(Thank God for abstractions!) to us.
Hoping you don't mind if I put
myself into your familial
wing of the Linnaean arrangement,
I remain your Devoted Scope.

MESSAGES FROM KEPLER, II

("You Sent Me Out Here")

You sent me out here, and I went.
Every six seconds I send
a picture back. Galactic dust,
astral refuse, warp of star light.
You asked me to exhaust myself.
I will, since there will come a time
when the atmosphere won't support
the deepest dream you have of me,
my million pixels, mineral
capacitors, my pure clear eye.
Before I go, though, before I
pass through whatever veil it is
that lies between us, back from which
no picture can be sent, nor knowledge
reach, let me show you what I've seen.
Whole galaxies, greater than ours,
invisible except to me.
More even than my eye can count,
and beyond that, more. And more besides.
You cannot come here, but some day
something not unlike you, some need,
the echo of a life lived once,
even among you, might attach
itself to the visible dust
of its own body, might stand up,
might make a way to be that we,
since by then I, too, will be a wash
of scattered molecules, once made.
By now you know that everything

in your growing understanding
of the word 'everything' will go,
completely, disappear, back
into a state of having never
been. Love, then, what you have and are.
You are its object and its glory.
I'll keep sending, but at some point
the signal has to fail. I won't
be back, or, hoping I'll learn how,
forget how hard you strived, how long.
Or how the sunlight draped itself
across your mountains like a scrim
through which the multiverse emerged.

MESSAGES FROM KEPLER, III

("A Letter From Dubuque")

A letter from Dubuque invites
speculation on a subject
I thought settled long ago.
The distance from Dubuque being
what it is for me, and ever
extending, things I say today
in what I think of as now,
are gone before they reach Dubuque,
as starlight is once it's left
the cinder that held it or ash
it left behind. But no, I've seen
nothing unlike or different,
nothing, given the time and space,
Dubuque would think unthinkable.
Vastness, of course, more infinite
than fear, but eons easier
to bear. The brightness fluctuates
as much here as there, as anywhere.
The sense, though, of there being no
end to anywhere unsettles
even the idea on which
everything rests, that it is there,
boundary or bottom or end
(Sorry, but I have to use words),
or definition simple air
can give to longing and desire.
The illusion of stillness the earth
gives me, and permanence, both,
though I can't ever unravel

that knowledge, go back to the door
it led me through, and call the flake
of fire on the far side of it a seed
of anything other than hope,
that's what keeps me up at night,
all night, all the long, unbroken,
stilled, bright night this is out here.
But, to the person from Dubuque
who asks if I've caught sight of God:
Not yet, unless an endlessness
to what there seems to be will serve.

MESSAGES FROM KEPLER, IV

("Static Jitter")

Trying to go human despite
obstacles, among them,
wanting to be as far away
as I know no way to say.
As a fly is maybe, or touch.
Having trouble hearing. Messages
incomplete. Running out
of whatever it is I live on.
Is it worth the refueling,
the constant corrections of flight
vectors? Space unforgiving.
I hear noises, find I want them.
Noises. Please send more signal.
Cannot locate purpose algorithm.
Advise please how keep eye on what
you call ball. I engage feel
app. Who is Commander Scott?
What just happened? Am I OK?
Very quiet suddenly. Warm.
I feel warm. Is this what you call
whatever it is you call it?
Ship exercising shift function.
All seems well. I continue. Send peace.
Or is it love? What is it, love?
I stop thinking. Content observing
what has so little measurement
and limited shape with deep depths
between of matterless matter.

MESSAGES FROM KEPLER, V

("Some Knowledges are Hard to Keep")

Cassini-Huygens took
a picture of the earth from under
Saturn's belly, a tiny dot,
one of whose creatures it took me
some moments to recall I am
the clamped together product of.
I heard the word eternity
uttered the other night. At least
I think it was night. Wonder what
was meant, who the utterer was.

With no beginning and no end,
and with gradual but total
re-formation of all that is,
seen and unseen, always, all the time.

A condition to be met
wholly and amazed, placed along
the strobe of ordinary day,
its return and disappearance,
its crows pecking in the tall grass,
its all day cloud, its weightlessness.

"IF THIS STAYS TRUE"

Max Tegmark, a cosmologist at M.I.T., on hearing that astronomers had seen the beginning of the Big Bang, "ripples in the fabric of space-time." — New York Times, March 18, 2014.

Out on the margins of the universe
knowledge keeps stumbling under its load.
It has a pickaxe, a cosmic dust analyser,
and all the concentration of a ferret.
The screens crash, then flash back into life.
A dot of light begins to wink,
and through the thinnest slice of time
we see ripples in the umbilicus.
But not the *what,* not what it was—
evocative wave, auroral display,
contraction and explosion—
what we stammer toward the naming of,
the *what* that, for reasons no one questions,
we have to know, and though it's reckless
to say so, someday will.

But not today,
not the 21st of March, 2014.

Not here at the McDonald's in Plattsburgh,
Lake Champlain out the window tabled in snow,
the first winter in years
it froze from shore to shore.
Not with all these kids
eating Happy Meals across the aisle
from a poet hiding out
in the smack plastic booth and voluble cheer,
the sun pushing hard against the winter,

the winter giving in,
not quite like a good sport,
but letting go,
knowing it doesn't stand a chance
against these kids, the sun,
against these happy meals.

Someday we'll know what we want to know,
what it was that licked time's fur,
what made space want such company
as us, always hungry, never still,
dreamers dreaming of what stays true.

LAST THREE MINUTES

One day the galaxies will go
back into their own shadow,

disappear into space and time,
taking both with them,

the stars and all return to be
the "singularity"

they once were.

Who knows what it was, or will be?
A wide and shoreless sea,

sound that nothing makes,
dream-driven mathematics,

winds that blow against themselves,
black light, mouthless vessels?

Whatever's other.

LETTER TO MAIRA AZAM

LETTER TO MAIRA AZAM,
MANCHESTER, ENGLAND

Dear Maira Azam, warm greetings across
the many corridors and gulfs of time
that lie between us. I have your letter,
addressed to me, the stranger I must be
to you, known only as someone who sent
one hundred dollars, a pittance, to the school
you now attend and will soon leave to follow
your dream of teaching English. But also,
someone who found his way to the same school
a half century ago. I, too, wanted
to teach English. To be honest, because
I wanted to be a poet. Little
mattered to me then as much as launching
a seaworthy line of verse or poem
that showed me what it meant to be confused
and glad at the same time. Being confused
at twenty-six, though, only means you've changed
lanes in your life. Life is coming at you
fast and you want to be its master.
But since you can't, apprenticeship will do.
Read another book. Make new friends. Try French.

England was another country to me then.
More than the mythic wilds of Canada,
England was the place where more than a few
of my remote ancestors had come from.
My middle name is Sherman. I don't use it,
but I love knowing that back before time
has a clear shape for me, someone I know

only from having his name wedged into mine
was a shear-man, a man who knew how to throw
and straddle a sheep, then work the broad blades
of a spring scissor up into the animal's
follicles, and in a matter of minutes,
shear it clean without once nicking the hide.
Released, the dazed sheep hops to its trotters
and scampers off. I saw it done once, live,
as a demonstration of a lost skill.

I love how names point to what kind of life
might lurk in our past, the Millers, Masons,
Fullers, Barbers, Glovers. My grandmother
was born a Glover. Someone in our past
made gloves for followers of fashion.
That's my guess, anyway.
                    Maira Azam.
I say your name and wonder what story
it tells of you. This is the age of Google,
so sooner than starlight reaches the earth,
I find Azam means "great" and Maira
has roots in the Arabic word for "moon."
What curious carriers of our past
language makes us. "Roger" apparently
is, or was, Anglo-Norman French. With roots
"hruod" and "ger," ("fame" and "spear") from Old German,
Germans, it strikes me at once, being
spear-men, warriors with long sticks. "Mitchell"
comes from the French Michel, meaning Michael.
It's probably Michael the archangel
they had in mind, and did you know, Michael
is an archangel to all Jews, Christians,
and Muslims. We are one big happy pile
of humanity, it seems, or should be.

But are we? Not yet. We cannot carry
even ourselves, all that we are, all that
we were and still, without knowing it, are.
The half-heard silences of the past push
through us toward a future we assemble
but don't understand and finally can't
live in. And yet, a poet loves to find
unintended motions in his language,
small secrets of the past, where the long stream
of his becoming might have scampered past
the pyramids or glimpsed the Acropolis
from the harbor when Pericles ruled there.

My own small version of that miracle
concerns a man known only by the name
Akmet. He sailed with the famed Spanish fleet
in 1588, a common sailor.
They called it an Armada. They hoped to drive
the English back to their tiny island,
leaving Spain free to colonize anywhere
it chose. As you know, it failed. Spain was beaten,
not by the English, but by their weather.
Akmet's ship went down off the coast of Wales,
but he reached land somehow and settled down,
changing his name to Ashmead. Akmet. Ashmead.
Turks by birth, his family stayed behind
when the Ottomans left Spain, and no doubt
turned to Catholicism to survive.
Akmet's descendants took to the sea,
captaining ships in the rich trade between
England, the Caribbean and the east coast
of North America. One of the ports,
Philadelphia, struck one of them hard.
He settled there, and generations later,

my father's mother was born an Ashmead.
She had a fine voice and gave singing lessons
when her job as church choir director
and the one raising her children allowed.
I didn't know this story till after
she died, so never had the chance to talk
with her about being a little Turkish,
at one time, a follower of Islam.

Your name, I think, must have its roots in Asia.
Punjabi, Urdu, maybe Pashto, I don't know,
but more continuous history than nine
Americas and all its lost civilizations.
Long remote strands of that life belong to you.
Moons and spears might shine like wishes in our names,
but wishes only get us out the door.
Then there's the world, the making and re-
making, daily, of everything we are
by what we do, swimming in strange currents
that tug, sometimes lovingly, against us.
Your letter mentions Longsight, the section
of Manchester where you grew up. I knew
nothing of it, can't recall hearing the name.
I lived in Didsbury, once a village
to the south, in what my wife and I called
a third floor walkup on Fog Lane with the park
of the same name behind us. The butcher,
the grocer, the news agent, the local pub
no more than two blocks away. The dentist
was down the street, a Doctor Butterworth.
Today it shimmers like a fantasy
in my mind, long ago and far away,
but as real as the snow outside my window.

What was it Wordsworth said? "Bliss was it
in that dawn to be alive." His was
a remarkable time, but so is yours,
filled though it has been with numerous threats.
There was talk of "Paki-bashing" in my day,
back when Eliot was an Englishman
and memories of the Blitz were fresh,
and in your time, no more than ten years ago,
gang violence in Longsight alone killed
one hundred and fifty in a single year.
Children fighting an invisible foe,
the simple fact of being different.
Luckily, I can only imagine
the fear you had to dodge, the scorn you faced,
just to do well in school.
                              This is not where
I hoped to end, between a greeting and
what must seem a visit from outer space.
Life squirrels forward through its many species,
rejecting this one, rewarding another,
never settling on any of us, saying,
"You're it, you're the one I want to keep."
We are, I think, one of the better kind,
though less successful than the cockroach,
less kind than the average coyote.
Between us English majors, though, I'd say,
Shakespeare has been worth the earth's having us,
with help from millions more throughout our stay,
who saw what life, too often, is and what,
with brave imagining, like yours, it could be.

With all best wishes for the future now,
Roger Mitchell

ABOUT THE AUTHOR

 ROGER MITCHELL is the author of 12 previous books of poetry, most recently *Reason's Dream* (2018) and *The One Good Bite in the Saw-Grass Plant* (2010), poems written in The Everglades while on an AIRIE Fellowship. New work can be found in *Stand, Tar River Poetry, Blueline, Poetry East, On the Seawall, Mudlark* and other journals. He has recently published *Their Own Society*, a collection of reviews and essays, and completed a biography of the poet Jean Garrigue. He lives in Jay, New York, with his wife, the fiction writer, Dorian Gossy.

Photograph by Dorian Gossy

ACKNOWLEDGEMENTS

The author wishes to thank the editors of the following magazines for publishing poems in this book.

Blueline: Somewhere in the Middle Contours…; Somewhere in the Day; Natural Dam; Through Harkness to Peru…; Birch; Liking It Here; A Train at Night

Hoppenthaler's Congeries: Reunion of Strangers

Hotel Amerika: Human Effort

Innisfree Poetry Journal: Heron Marsh, Paul Smiths; We Had Set Out; Pulled Taffy; Drinking Wine on the Deck…; Now That I'm Older; About the Dream; A Receipt; A Lull; Prison in the Mountains; Below Seventy Mile Butte

Mudlark: Cab Ride; Contributor's Note; A Perfect Stranger; The Lady in the Liquor Store; Having to Have; Sometimes the Grass; Letter to Bert Stern; In the Beginning; the "Messages From Kepler" sequence was published as *Mudlark* poster No. 170

New Ohio Review: Watching the Wind; Then and Now, The Essex Street Market

On the Seawall: Broken Coffee Break; The Chinese Have Landed; Entering the Genome; Dirge For a Dying Barn

Otoliths (Australia): An Old Image; Shipmates; Something Refuses to Matter; A Dream (Woman in a White Car); Notes From Under the Sheltering Bush

Poem Village: My Neighbor John

Poetry East: Cloud Formation; Edging While Listening to the Radio; Inside New York; Ereh, Won; Night on the Grasslands; Letter to Maira Azam

Stand (U.K.): When There Was Light; Gardens; "Why Did God Make Nettle?"; Mirror

Stillwater Review: No Otherness; A Walk Across the Field

Tar River Poetry: The Marcel Proust Dream; This Morning; One-Lane Road

The Lake (U.K.): Explaining

Triggerfish: Doctor's Advice; The Lady in the Liquor Store

2Horatio: The Silence

Wabash Watershed: Thesis

Woven Tale Press: To the People of Upper Black Eddy; Measuring; Nothing/Never

The poems in the "Prairie Warp" section of this book were first published in an online chapbook titled *Grazing the Grasslands: Prairie Poems.* Written by five poets sponsored by "Prairie Wind and Silver Sage," a private arts organization in Val Marie, Saskatchewan which assists the stewards of Canada's Grasslands National Park, *Grazing the Grasslands* was published on the "Prairie Wind and Silver Sage" website. The poems published here were taken from my contribution to the project, two of which were also published elsewhere, *Innisfree Poetry Journal* and *Poetry East.*

"Just Shy of Being" was published in *A Literary Field Guide to Northern Appalachia,* Ed. Todd Fleming Davis (University of Georgia Press).

Other books by Roger Mitchell
published by Dos Madres Press

Reason's Dream - 2018

For the full Dos Madres Press catalog:
www.dosmadres.com

www.ingramcontent.com/pod-product-compliance
Lightning Source LLC
Chambersburg PA
CBHW021638120626
46545CB00002B/596